Agenda for the Study of Macroeconomic Policy

This is one of several papers that have developed
from the American Enterprise Institute's
1981–1982 Contemporary Economic Problems project.
The eleven papers of that project completed in 1981
were published earlier in a joint volume, as future contributions
to the Contemporary Economic Problems project will be. The titles
of the 1981–1982 studies being published individually are:

Politics versus Markets:
International Differences in Macroeconomic Policies
Stanley W. Black

Current Problems of Monetary Policy:
Would the Gold Standard Help?
Phillip Cagan

The Employment of Immigrants in the United States
Barry R. Chiswick

The High-Employment Budget and Potential Output:
A Critique Focusing on Two Recent Contributions
William Fellner

Progress of Economic Reform in the People's Republic of China
D. Gale Johnson

Interindustry Differences in Productivity Growth
John W. Kendrick

Patterns of Regional Economic Decline and Growth:
The Past and What Has Been Happening Lately
Mark Perlman

Agenda for the Study of Macroeconomic Policy
Herbert Stein

American Enterprise Institute

Agenda for the Study of Macroeconomic Policy

Herbert Stein

A Study in Contemporary Economic Problems, 1982
William Fellner, Project Director

Agenda for the Study of Macroeconomic Policy

Herbert Stein

A Study in
Contemporary Economic Problems, 1982
William Fellner, Project Director

American Enterprise Institute
Washington and London

Herbert Stein is editor of *The AEI Economist;* A. Willis Robertson Professor of Economics, University of Virginia; former chairman, President's Council of Economic Advisers; and senior fellow at the American Enterprise Institute.

Library of Congress Cataloging in Publication Data

Stein, Herbert, 1916—
    Agenda for the study of macroeconomic policy.
    (A Study in contemporary economic problems) (AEI
studies ; 376)
    1. United States—Economic policy—1981—
I. Title. II. Series. III. Series: AEI studies ; 376.
HC106.8.S74   1982   339.5'0973   83-2513

ISBN 0–8447–3516–7

AEI Studies 376

Printed in the United States of America

Agenda for the Study of Macroeconomic Policy

As the 1970s came to an end, it appeared that the poor economic performance of the preceding fifteen years, accompanied by new economic analysis, had led to a revolution of thinking about macroeconomic policy and would lead to a revolution of practice. The revolution could be most simply described as anti-Keynesian and pro-monetarist, but other adjectives had to be invoked to give its full flavor. Those adjectives included "supply-side," "anti-government," and "anti-intellectual," or at least "anti-intellectual-pretensions," meaning great skepticism of claims to ability to understand, predict, and manipulate the performance of the economy.

More specifically, the revolution rejected the notion that the proper central strategy of economic policy was the discretionary, "fine-tuning" management of the federal budget to keep aggregate demand at a level that would maintain full employment. Instead the revolution called for stabilization of the money supply to provide a stable and predictable overall economic environment in which private market forces would bring employment and output to their "natural" or "equilibrium" level, whatever that might be. The revolution rejected or at least deemphasized government measures to redistribute the national income in favor of low-income people or other preferred objects and emphasized government policies, mainly negative, to make the national income grow more rapidly.

The impact on policy of this revolution in economic thinking was already evident in the Carter administration. In October 1979 the Federal Reserve announced a change of strategy that was generally understood to be a major step toward more emphasis on controlling the growth of the money supply to make it steadier and slower. The president and Congress took steps to reduce the taxes believed to bear most heavily on investment and productivity. The rise of government spending was slowed. When the deficits implied in President Carter's budget of January 1980 seemed to shock the financial markets, he proposed revisions designed to reduce them. The recession of 1980 was accepted without expansive fiscal action.

But it was natural to expect the revolution in economic policy to be carried on much more radically in the Reagan administration. (Reagan would be Lenin to Carter's Kerensky.) He had used the anti-Keynesian, monetarist, supply-side, anti-government language in extreme form during the campaign. After his inauguration the language continued and was translated into action to an unusual degree. A specific path of restrained monetary growth was made part of the administration's program in a way that had not been seen before. An unprecedented tax cut was enacted. It was accompanied by expenditure reductions that were large in relation to common expectations of political feasibility, though not in relation to the size of the tax cut. Devotion to a balanced budget was reaffirmed, and a long-run budget plan was laid out that would bring the budget into balance by 1984. The administration's determination to shun the past course of "stop and go," "fine-tuning" fiscal policy was emphatically, and disdainfully, restated.

But at what might have been the moment of great triumph for the new economics, questions flooded in again, and consensus began to dissolve. Uncertainties appeared in both monetary and fiscal policy. Although the major change in Federal Reserve policy had promised more stable growth in the quantity of money, in fact the money supply was more volatile after the change than before. Once this became apparent, more attention had to be paid to the question whether this volatility had serious consequences. Although strong claims were made about this, the answer was not clear, and the general propositions about monetary policy that constituted the revolution did not imply how much volatility over what periods was consistent with "stable" monetary policy. Moreover, questions arose about whether, if a much higher degree of short-run stability was needed, failure to achieve it was due to inadequacy of the control instruments or to something else or was inevitable. The period of the new, stabilizing monetary policy was also a period of unusual change in the composition of the public's moneylike assets, which raised questions about the reliability of the relations between overall economic behavior and the quantity of some particular "money." These questions about conventional monetarism kept alive interest in an entirely different version of anti-Keynesian monetary policy— the gold standard. In the fall of 1982 the Federal Reserve announced a "temporary" relaxation of its previous devotion to announced targets for the money supply, a devotion that critics claimed had never been very great. The significance of this deviation was unclear except that it both reflected and raised questions about the adequacy of the monetary rules by which we had been guided.

So after about two years the meaning and validity of monetarism were much less clear than they had seemed when it was only an idea in opposition to prevailing practice. There was a similar development on the fiscal side. In fact, it turned out that merely rejecting Keynesian fine-tuning did not constitute a prescription for fiscal policy. The natural alternative to the Keynesian policy was balancing the budget, and that was how the new fiscal policy was conventionally described. But once the revolution was installed, the difficulty of balancing the budget in practice became evident, and the question arose whether balancing the budget was imperative, or was sufficiently important to require the painful steps needed to achieve it, or, indeed, mattered at all. The reversal of roles on this question was illuminating. In the political realm, many of the people who had been the stoutest champions of balancing the budget previously, when they were out of office, began to find sophisticated arguments for not balancing; whereas those who had been defenders of deficits for almost fifty years discovered the virtues of the old-time religion of the balanced budget. This led some cynics to the view that there never had been anything to the balanced-budget idea but a stick with which the outs could beat the ins.

But if budget balancing was not a useful principle and Keynesian functional finance was out, what did we have for guidance on fiscal policy? And even if one did think there was something in budget balancing, there were unanswered questions about what it meant. People who had once rejected the idea of "balancing the budget at high employment" as a subterfuge, or as unworthy compromising with the Keynesians, had to recognize that balancing the budget could not mean balancing the budget all the time regardless of economic conditions. But what were the conditions, if any, in which it should be balanced? This became a glaring issue as it became obvious that seemingly minor changes in the economic assumptions on which budget projections were calculated could do more to change the apparent size of deficits than painful decisions about tax rates and expenditure programs. So the whole debate about the budget took on an unreal look, concerned with numbers based on assumptions that could not be checked even in retrospect.

Moreover, as attention turned to the question whether deficits mattered, a number of different reasons for being concerned about deficits emerged. But then it appeared that corresponding to every reason for being concerned about the deficit was a different definition of the deficit that was relevant. So the notion of balancing "the" budget became as complicated as the notion of stabilizing "the" money supply.

To add to the list of causes for uncertainty about the meaning and validity of the new macroeconomic policy, the common-sense view that one way to reduce a deficit was to increase taxes and raise the revenue was forcefully attacked. Two quite different objections were raised to the common-sense view. One was that raising tax rates reduces the revenue, by reducing the taxable national income. This interesting hypothesis led to puzzlement about why we had any taxes at all, since no one seemed to like them. The other objection was that raising tax rates would indeed raise the revenue but that the government would spend any additional revenue, so that raising the rates would not reduce the deficit. In this view, the deficit was not a policy variable, but was given by some political force. In the summer of 1982 the administration seemed to return to the old-fashioned idea that raising taxes was a way to reduce the deficit, but it did so apologetically, and many of its supporters did not agree.

Earlier thinking had been that the expenditure side of the budget was too encrusted with particular programmatic considerations to be used as an instrument of macroeconomic policy, a role that had to be left to the revenue side of the budget. Now it was held that the revenue side of the budget was useless for that purpose.

To add one more without exhausting the list of reasons for uncertainty about the state of macroeconomics, the experience of 1981–1982 opened wide the question of the relation between restraint of the nominal side of the economy and the behavior of the real output and employment side. The hopeful view at the beginning of 1981 had been that a policy of monetary restraint, publicly accepted with sufficient credibility, could reduce the rate of growth of nominal GNP and the price level without any adverse effect on output and employment, or at least without any serious adverse effect. In 1981 we had an announced change of fiscal and monetary policy in a disinflationary direction, in what would have seemed the most favorable political conditions for achieving credibility. But the slow-down of nominal GNP growth and inflation then realized was accompanied by an unusually large decline of output and rise of unemployment. What did this imply about the steps needed to achieve credibility, or about the credibility theory itself?

This state of confusion and skepticism about the new macroeconomics is not surprising. Putting the new theory into operation would obviously require answering many specific questions that did not have to be answered when we were talking about big, general, largely negative ideas. The process of selling the new ideas inevitably involved making more extravagant claims for them than could ever be fulfilled. For this reason, all "new ideas" once installed will be disappointing. Economic discussion is political discussion, at least when the discussion reaches the public. Once the new ideas were applied, they became objects of political attack on a greater scale than previously. And once the new ideas became the slogans of the party in office, they acquired responsibility for all the ills the economy suffered, whether that responsibility was legitimate or not. The new ideas, moreover, were basically ideas about how to keep the economy in a state of equilibrium. They were stabilizing ideas. They did not have much to say about how to get to equilibrium from a condition of high inflation, with its accompanying expectations and constraints, and high unemployment.

The present uncertainty about the new macroeconomics does not mean that it is invalid. Still less does it mean that we should return to the naive Keynesian liberalism of the Kennedy-Johnson days. With the passage of time and with constructive discussion, some of the questions would be answered, some of the expectations would be moderated, and if the policy was only fairly successful, the transitional difficulties would be left behind.

Still, the current uncertainty about the meaning and validity of the new macroeconomic policy that became the nation's standard doctrine at the end of the 1970s presents dangers. First, there is the obvious danger that seriously wrong decisions will be made. Even if this should be escaped, the economy suffers from lack of knowledge about what policy is coming next and from lack of confidence in whatever policy may eventuate. Some of the economic problems of 1982 are due to unusual uncertainty about what fiscal and monetary policy will be in the next several years and what the effects of that policy will be, rather than to current errors of policy or to a settled conviction that policy will be wrong in the future.

There is great need to resolve the uncertainties that now exist. That means more than that economists need to learn the answers to the unsettled questions about macroeconomics. Of course they need to do that. But the fact must be accepted that this learning is going to come slowly. Meanwhile, the country must learn what to do in the state of limited knowledge—which is our perpetual condition. More than that, we must seek a consensus on policy, because predictable stability of policy may be more important than the "best" policy, and predictable stability requires that there be some agreement. Otherwise, policy is a political football, which may change direction radically after any election or in anticipation of any election.

The present situation of uncertainty and disagreement about macroeconomic policy is reminiscent of the situation around the end of World War II. The country had been through a decade of disastrous economic failure. We were determined not to repeat that. But we also knew that the country had not found the formula for dealing with the depression, even after ten years. The war had only declared an intermission in that effort. There were people who thought they knew what needed to be done, but in fact what they knew was very general—an attitude rather than an operational program—and there was wide disagreement about the attitude.

By that time, the latter days of World War II, the predominant viewpoint in the economics profession was Keynesian. The Keynesians thought they had the key to our economic problem—use of fiscal policy (which meant government spending) to sustain adequate demand and so maintain full employment—but they were only beginning to recognize the economic, administrative, and political difficulties of carrying out such a program. There were a number of economists who, having originally been sympathetic, had fallen off the Keynesian bandwagon when they saw the extremes to which the Keynesian enthusiasts were going. These dissenters gave considerable weight to money—the term monetarist had not yet been invented—but they had no specific plan for the management of money. There were still fundamentalists around who believed that the depression had been caused by the New Deal and that the needed course was to get the government out of the economy—whatever that meant for fiscal and monetary policy. There were others who took from the wartime management of the economy the lesson that similar management would be needed in peacetime. And there were still others who knew only that something had to be done to keep the country from sliding back into depression.

When the United States entered the war, no one could tell what postwar economic policy would be like. But within a few years after the war ended, a substantial consensus had been achieved, a consensus on policy that worked fairly well and survived for about fifteen years. An unusual national discussion of economic policy contributed to this result. There was a widespread awareness of the existence of a major national economic problem and a general desire to participate in the search for a solution. The discussion was addressed to long-run issues rather than to immediate decisions, but the discussion of long-run issues had an unusually large practical and operational content. Moreover, the discussion rose above partisan and parochial interest to an unusual degree.

Some specific components of this discussion may be listed to indicate its character:

- the statements of the Committee for Economic Development, an organization of businessmen established specifically for the purpose of formulating economic policy for postwar America
- statements of the National Planning Association—representing business, labor, agriculture, and academic experts
- unusually thoughtful statements of their position by the Chamber of Commerce and the National Association of Manufacturers
- a contest, sponsored by the Pabst Brewing Company, for essays on how to maintain postwar employment, in which there were 46,000 entries and national publicity
- writing by several leading economists on macroeconomic strategies, notably Friedman's "Monetary and Fiscal Framework" and a symposium, "Financing American Prosperity," published by the Twentieth Century Fund
- reports of two task forces established by the American Economic Association
- the hearings and discussion on the legislation that was finally called the Employment Act of 1946
- the hearings on economic policy held by a subcommittee of the Joint Economic Committee under the chairmanship of Senator Paul H. Douglas

The national discussion, of which these were only the most conspicuous parts, led to a national consensus. As I have written elsewhere, it domesticated Keynes and liberated monetary policy. It led to a normal rule of budget policy: balancing the budget at high employment. It established the revenue side of the budget as the main instrument for stabilization policy, defined the unified budget as the relevant measure, and identified 4 percent unemployment as the standard of high employment. Monetary policy was recognized as an equal partner and freed from the commitment to fixing interest rates. The Council of Economic Advisers and the Joint Economic Committee were created to advise the president and the Congress.

This consensus, we can see now, was not ideal. Still, it was great progress from where we stood in 1939 or 1945. And there was sufficient agreement to provide reasonable stability and predictability of policy for some time.

What we need now is not a return to the postwar policy consensus but a return to the postwar discussion process—and we are not getting it. The utterances of economists, with few exceptions, are either incomprehensible or incredible. Political discussion is myopic and intensely partisan. The statements of business organizations and of other special-interest groups are simply that—expressions of special interest. The validity of these observations can be checked by comparing any issue of the *American Economic Review* for 1982 with any issue for 1947, by comparing any current statement of any business organization today with those of the Committee for Economic Development thirty to forty years ago, or by comparing the discussion of the Employment Act of 1946 with the discussion of the Full Employment Act of 1978 (the Humphrey-Hawkins Act).

There are undoubtedly many reasons for the difference in the quality of the postwar discussion and the present discussion. Our present problem is intellectually and politically more difficult than the problem envisaged in 1945. Then we were overwhelmingly concerned with the simple problem of full employment. Today we know that we have a complex problem of inflation, growth, full employment, efficiency, welfare or justice, and freedom. Economists, having become more sophisticated, are more aware of the limits of their knowledge and in their scientific roles more reluctant to give advice, whatever may be true in their political, publicist roles.

But there is, in my opinion, one chief explanation for the difference between 1945, say, and 1982. In 1945 the country had been through the agony of the Great Depression and the great war. There was a generation of leaders who were acutely aware that the nation could be in mortal peril. They accepted the responsibility to make the intellectual effort and the moral effort—to rise above their ideological commitments and private interests—in order to save the nation. That feeling seems rare today. Perhaps our economic condition is not yet critical enough. But we should not have to experience disaster before turning seriously and objectively to dealing with economic policy issues.

The obvious contradictions of policy in 1982—the difference between our professions and our realizations in fiscal and monetary policy and the related worries about a depression or revived inflation—may provide some stimulus for the needed discussion. There are hopeful signs. The annual report of the Council of Economic Advisers issued in February 1982 wrestled with the meaning of budget balancing in a constructive way. The Gold Commission recommended a congressional study of rules of monetary policy, which could be the occasion for trying to synthesize present thinking about money. Even the proposal for a constitutional amendment requiring a balanced budget shows awareness of the current problem and, although it is not in my opinion a good idea, may precipitate serious discussion of the principles of budget policy we really mean to live with.

But the kind of discussion we need will depend basically on the private sector. Government agencies and congressional committees can provide a forum, but they cannot rise above the quality of thinking that goes on in the private sector. There is need for private research bodies, organizations of business, labor, and other sectors, and individual economists to try to make the leap to a more constructive, durable, objective formulation of policy, which might have general acceptability.

Questions for Consideration

In the remainder of this paper I discuss what seem to me the main questions about macroeconomic policy on which attention needs to be focused and answers need to be sought. I want to make clear that I am not primarily proposing an agenda for research, but an agenda for thinking, discussing, agreeing, and deciding. Of course, more research is needed and would be welcome in the process I am describing. But the fruits of research in this field will come slowly. Our urgent need is to try to bring the present state of knowledge to bear and to decide open-mindedly what to do in the limited state of our knowledge.

Is There Macroeconomics, and What Is It? The notion that there is a macroeconomic policy that differs from other aspects of economic policy implies that there are certain "overall" policy instruments, which have an effect on the "overall" behavior of the economy in ways that other instruments do not and which affect only the "overall" behavior of the economy. As an extreme example, one might say that the quantity of money determines the price level and only that, relative prices being unaffected, and that nothing else influences the price level. But we know that the world is not really like that. All the instruments that we conventionally consider macroinstruments have microeffects; that is, they affect the allocation of output and the distribution of income. And at least a great many of the instruments that we do not conventionally consider macroinstruments do have effects on such overall aspects of the economy as total output, nominal GNP, or the price level.

The fuzziness of the distinction between macro- and micropolicy is clearest in fiscal policy. We usually think of total government expenditures, total tax revenues, and the difference between them—the deficit or surplus—as macroinstruments. But it is hard to think of a statement about the effects of these aggregates that might not also be true of some subaggregates. One might say, for example, that the choice between taxing and borrowing is a macroeconomic decision, which has an effect on the overall rate of economic growth. But to some degree a choice between consumption taxes and income taxes has such an effect, and choices among forms of income tax do also. Moreover, the choice between taxing and borrowing does not have only overall effects on the economy. The choice will, for example, affect Oregon and Michigan differently from California and Florida. Different kinds of taxes or expenditures or methods of managing the debt have different macroeffects, and different actions about the budget aggregates have different microeffects.

The same thing is true, though probably not to the same degree, of monetary policy. Change in the rate of growth of the money supply, usually regarded as the macroinstrument in the monetary field, does not affect only the price level or some other macrovariable. At least in the short run it will affect the distribution of income and output. We could also have, and sometimes have had, policy instruments to control separately the quantity of different kinds of financial assets, and the use of these instruments would have macroeffects as well as microeffects.

If economists knew all about everything, there would be no need for the distinction between macroeconomic policy and microeconomic policy. There would be one enormous model of the economy into which all possible policy actions could be plugged and from which all possible consequences could be read out and the combination of actions that maximized some social objective could be calculated. But, of course, economists do not know everything.

At this point there are two alternatives. One is to try to do our best as if we did know everything or at least would bring to bear on every decision everything we know, however little, about all its consequences. In deciding whether to build the B-1 bomber or refit the B-52s, we would consider the effects of the decision on the general price level. In deciding whether to raise the money supply by 5 percent or 6 percent, we would consider the effect of the decision on the relative prices of corn and lima beans in South Succotash.

The other alternative is, when trying to affect the overall objectives, to focus on those instruments that we believe *mainly* affect those objectives, even though we recognize that other instruments also have *some* overall effect. When trying to decide on the use of those instruments, we would focus on their overall effects, even though we recognize that they also have some other effects. This would be a recognition that if we try to think of everything at the same time, we will not make good decisions. If we tried to stabilize the price level by thinking of all the things that affect the price level, we would be bogged down in decisions of great uncertainty and little relevance.

Probably most people would agree that the second alternative is the only workable one. Yet it is surprising how many people, when asked to think "fundamentally" about the causes of inflation and its cures, for example, come up with lists of scores of demographic, psychological, political, and technological factors. This is more likely to be true of "practical" people than of economists.

Adopting the second alternative means accepting the fact that macroeconomics and macroeconomic policy are abstractions made for pragmatic reasons, because we cannot think of everything at the same time. Thus it is no serious objection to a macroeconomic policy that it leaves out of account some instruments or some effects—unless those instruments or effects are so important that leaving them out of account worsens the decision-making process. Moreover, this way of looking at macroeconomic policy already implies a partial answer to the perennial question about rules versus discretion. That is, if "discretion" means that all possible information must be taken into account in making every decision, the idea that there is macroeconomics means the rejection of discretion because it calls for concentrating on a certain kind of information in making certain decisions.

In fact, the notion of discretion in the sense just mentioned is unrealistic. No person or organization can make decisions by continuously taking in "all" information and processing it in all possible ways. Everyone operates by some decision-making rules, conscious or unconscious, that limit the information to be taken into account and its use. The argument about rules is an argument about which rules—how simple, explicit, and durable—and from whom they come.

It is significant that the 1936 essay by Henry Simons that precipitated the discussion of rules was called not "Rules versus Discretion in Monetary Policy" but "Rules versus Authority in Monetary Policy." It was really about *whose* rules—Simons's or the authority's. When people outside the government argue for rules, they are arguing for the imposition of their rules on the authorities. When people inside the government argue against rules, they are arguing for their own rules, which they may not even be able to describe.

What we seek is a set of instruments and objectives that are so much more closely related to each other than to other instruments and objectives that we can draw a line around them and call them macroeconomics. The possibility and difficulty of doing this become clearer if we distinguish between "nominal" macroeconomics and "real" macroeconomics. Nominal macroeconomics consists of the relations between certain instruments and nominal objectives—nominal GNP or the price level. Concern with these nominal objectives does not mean that we are not interested in the real magnitudes—output, employment, and unemployment. It means that in this compartment we are interested in the real magnitudes insofar as they are influenced by the nominal magnitudes. What seems to me the realistic version of this is that we are concerned with the effects on the real magnitudes that result from the instability and unpredictability of the nominal magnitudes. There may be other ways to describe this relationship, but I am not concerned with them here.

With respect to nominal macroeconomics, it does seem possible to identify a limited number of instruments that are distinctly more important than any others and whose nominal macroeconomic effects are much more important than any other effects they have. Thus decisions about the size of the money supply clearly belong in the compartment of nominal macroeconomics, whereas decisions about the B-1 bomber do not, even though producers of B-1 bombers may have propensities to hold money that are different from other people's. One could say that nominal macroeconomic policy consists of the management of the money supply to achieve certain objectives with respect to nominal GNP or the price level—say, stability and predictability.

A problem arises with respect to fiscal policy. We are used to thinking of fiscal and monetary policy as being the instruments of macroeconomics. Whether fiscal policy has any important effect on nominal variables is a disputed question, much less likely to be answered in the affirmative today than thirty years ago. But even if fiscal policy does have an important effect on the nominal variables, it does not necessarily belong in the compartment of nominal macroeconomics. Anything fiscal policy can do about the nominal variables monetary policy may be able to do with fewer other effects, that is, fewer real effects. In that case fiscal policy does not have to be assigned to the nominal compartment, but can be determined in relation to its other effects.

One possibility is that aspects of fiscal policy can be divided between the nominal and the real compartments. It may be that what is important about fiscal policy for the nominal objectives is the short-time variation of fiscal measures whereas what is important for the real objectives is the long-term level and trend. In that case the short-time variations might be put in the nominal compartment and the long-term level and trend in the real compartment.

12

Of course, there is no necessary reason why the same instrument should not be involved in both compartments. That would complicate decision making, but nothing says it has to be simple. It may, indeed, produce irreconcilable conflicts. Suppose it were true, which I do not believe but can conceive, that satisfactory development of the nominal variables required a large budget deficit but that satisfactory development of the real variables required a large budget surplus. The public wants to hold government securities equal to a constant fraction of nominal GNP as nominal GNP grows, but a high rate of private investment requires that private savings be supplemented by a government surplus. There could then be a difficult choice to be made.

The puzzling questions arise, however, when one thinks about what objectives and instruments belong in the compartment of "real macroeconomics."

The problem is that there seem to be in the real world no single dominant objective and no single dominant instrument related to it. In the nominal world there is a dominant macro-objective, which is predictability. One cannot conceive of a policy with respect to the nominal world that does not aim at predictability. That seems to be the maximum that nominal policy can provide and the minimum it should offer. In the long run, predictable nominal behavior will yield the best real results that nominal behavior can yield. Moreover, even if it might be useful and feasible, it does not seem "right" that the government should follow a policy of misleading the public, which is what would be involved in a policy that did not aim at predictability. This still leaves questions of just what is to be predictable, on what path, and how the predictability is to be achieved, which will be discussed below. But at least one can define in a general way what the objective of nominal macroeconomic policy is. And, as already stated, one can identify an instrument that has a strong comparative advantage in achieving that objective.

In the real macroeconomy there are a number of objectives, none of which seems to dominate all others, and a number of instruments, each of which affects a number of objectives and none of which seems to have a superior relation to any single objective. What we are concerned with here is fiscal policy, or whether there is any such thing. The basic notion of fiscal policy is that there are a few aggregate magnitudes of the budget, or possibly only one, that have effects so important and exceptional that decisions about these aggregates should dominate decisions about their components. This notion is implicit in the federal budget process and in the division between "fiscal policy" and "public finance" in university curricula and elsewhere. The most obvious example is the idea of the size of the deficit or surplus as an overriding consideration to which other policies had to be accommodated. This was, of course, implicit in the idea that balancing the budget was a principle to which decisions about particular expenditures and taxes must conform. It was also implicit in the simpler and more operational version of the functional finance rule. There was some deficit or surplus that would be optimum for full employment, and expenditure and revenue decisions had to be adapted to that. Everyone knew that was not literally true and that the optimum size of the deficit depended on the level of expenditures as well as on the composition of both the expenditures and the revenues. But the discussion proceeded as if that could be ignored.

We have passed beyond the idea that the budget-balancing rule was handed down from Mount Sinai, however, and we have also left functional finance behind us. It is now much less clear than it seemed that one can arrive at a decision about the size of deficits or surpluses that is independent of and prior to decisions about the particulars of the budget. We have to ask what objective is to be served by the choice of the size of deficit or surplus. Probably the answer that would most commonly be given to that question today is that the decision has something to do with economic growth. The larger the surplus, the more funds are available for private investment and the higher will be the rate of economic growth. But this provides no unique guide to the size of the surplus or deficit that is so clear and imperative that other budget decisions must be adapted to it. For one thing, the desirable rate of growth is something to be decided. We obviously do not want the maximum possible rate of growth. Economic growth has its costs, and beyond some point more of it is not worth the cost. Moreover, even if we knew what the optimum rate of growth was or what the optimum contribution to growth was, there would be various packages of budgetary policies and other policies that would achieve it. The budget surplus would be only one ingredient in those packages. Thus in the early 1960s there was a "liberal" budget strategy for economic growth, which involved, paradoxically, large budget surpluses, high taxes, especially on the rich, and increasing expenditures for "human capital"—education, training, and labor mobility. This strategy, which was clearest in the writings of James Tobin, was never implemented, probably because the high-tax element was politically impossible to carry through. Today we have a "conservative" budget strategy for economic growth, which involves large budget deficits, tax incentives for private saving, and even greater tax incentives, including in some circumstances negative tax rates, for certain kinds of investment—business plant and equipment. The 1960 policy was a low-interest-rate strategy; the 1980 policy is a high-interest-rate strategy. Probably some desired contribution to growth could be achieved by either of these strategies, but the outcome would differ in important respects, notably in the distribution of income by size and in the size of the government sector.

The point is that even if some given growth goal were accepted as the object of fiscal policy, and even as an objective superior to all others, that would not enable us to say that the budget surplus must be such-and-such and that other budget decisions must be accommodated to that. There would be various policy packages involving different budget surpluses or deficits that would yield the growth result, and a choice among these policy packages would have to be made on the basis of their effect on other objectives. And these other objectives are important—defense, size of government, income distribution, claim of individuals to dispose of their own earned incomes, at least. Moreover, it is unrealistic to think that a goal for economic growth could be sensibly chosen without consideration of the means by which it was to be achieved—whether, for example, by cutting defense or by severe limitation of the ability of income earners to conserve their own income.

What has been said here about the idea that the connection between surpluses and growth provides a precise and overriding answer to the proper size of the surplus applies also to a more recent view of the connection between taxes and growth. This view is simply that taxes should be reduced where they impede growth. There are two problems with this. One is that the analysis is usually partial. Except in the unlikely cases where tax reduction raises the revenue, tax reduction involves, arithmetically, tax increases elsewhere or expenditure decreases or deficit increases. And these consequences will have effects on growth that may make the total policy negative from the standpoint of growth. There will also be effects other than the growth effect, which must be considered in deciding on the merits of the policy.

This discussion helps us to understand the meaning of "supply-side" economics and to see what is valid and what is invalid about it. The relevant distinction is between the nominal economy and the real economy, not between the demand side and the supply side. (I sometimes regret having coined the term "supply side.") The supply-siders reject the use of fiscal policy to affect the nominal variables, notably nominal total income. That is because they think that fiscal policy does not affect nominal income, or because they think that fiscal policy cannot be used efficiently for that purpose, or because they think that the behavior of nominal income does not affect the real economy. So they believe that fiscal policy should concentrate on the real economy directly. This seems to be a defensible position. The difficulties arise in understanding the relations of fiscal policy to the real economy. There, it seems to me, several mistakes have been made, though not all by all supply-siders:

• Overestimating the "partial" effects of particular tax or expenditure changes on total output or its rate of growth. The partial effects are the effects that would occur if all other taxes, expenditures, and the surplus or deficit were unchanged, which is impossible except under quite unlikely circumstances.

• Neglecting or underestimating the significance of the repercussions of particular tax changes on other elements of the budget. Most important, this meant neglecting the adverse effect on the growth of output that might result from the deficits that tax reductions would cause.

• Underestimating the importance from the standpoint of the supply of output of the differences among types of taxes and objects of expenditure. There is a tendency to consider all taxes or, in some formulations, all expenditures equally as a "wedge" between production and the income that is an incentive to produce.

• Neglecting aspects of the real economy other than the supply of output that are legitimate and necessary concerns of economics and economic policy.

What was wrong with supply-side economics was not that it discarded the last remnants of the Keynesian idea of using fiscal policy to manage the nominal economy. It was an unrealistic and oversimplified view of what was entailed in using fiscal policy to manage the real economy.

We have many objectives in the real economy, and many of these objectives must be balanced against one another. That is, we do not want as much growth, or as much income equality, or as little government, or even as much defense as we can get. There are trade-offs among the various objectives, and the amount of any one that is desirable depends on its cost in terms of the others. Moreover, the amount of any one objective that it is worth giving up to get some of another objective will be appraised differently by different people and cannot be determined in any mechanical way. These trade-offs have to be valued in a political process, and the valuation will change from time to time. The government has a number of instruments, not all in the domain of fiscal policy, that affect the achievement of these objectives. Many of the instruments affect several objectives, and most of the objectives are affected by a variety of instruments.

The upshot of this is that it does not seem possible to make reasonable decisions about any of the big aggregates of the budget—say, the deficit or total spending or total revenues—without regard to the decisions made about the other aggregates or without regard to the components of the aggregates or without regard to several objectives, not only one. If this thought is carried to its logical extreme, it calls for simultaneous decisions with regard to all budgetary instruments and objectives. The decision whether to build the B-1 bomber or Stealth would affect the income of people in Kansas and therefore would have to be made in the light of what agricultural price support policy is doing to the price of wheat, but that would affect the real incomes of poor families in the Bronx and would have to be decided in the light of the appropriation for aid to families with dependent children, and so on. But that, as we said at the outset, is impossible and also means that there is no such thing as macroeconomic policy.

It is necessary to find some practical level of aggregation at which decisions can be made that would dominate decisions made at lower levels. All that is being suggested here is that the sensible procedure might not permit a prior decision about total deficit or total expenditures or total receipts, or all three of them together. One could imagine a somewhat lower level of aggregation at which the fiscal instruments might be:

> total defense expenditures
> total income assistance expenditures
> total investment expenditures (human and physical capital)
> interest
> other expenditures
> revenues from proportional taxation
> revenues from progressive taxation
> other revenues
> deficit or surplus (by subtraction)

Decisions could be made about these aggregates in terms of their effect on economic growth, national security, income distribution, dominance of government, and consumption by income earners. Once these decisions had been made, decisions at a lower level—navy versus army, education versus dams, and so on—would be adapted to them.

The foregoing is meant as an illustration, not as a proposal. It comes fairly close to the categories in which the public discussion of the first budget resolution in 1982 ran. There was then, however, a tendency for the discussion and decisions to be "tainted" by reference to subordinate details. Moreover, the relation between the instruments and the objectives was much less explicit than it might have been.

The illustration may serve, however, to point up two difficulties. One is the problem of choosing the efficient level of aggregation. It is aways possible to say that we could decide on total defense expenditures better if we knew how much was for strategic weapons, and could decide how much to spend for strategic weapons better if we knew how much was for the MX, and how much to spend for the MX better if we knew where it was to be based, and so on. But that way lie frustration and madness. The problem is to choose a level of decision making where the value of the additional information that would be provided by more detail does not equal the cost in loss of ability to weigh the big issues. There is a point at which one cannot see the forest for the trees.

Some presidents have been justly criticized for paying so much attention to the details of the budget that they lose sight of the most important choices. They fall into this error probably not because they want more information in order to decide the basic questions but because of failure to see the basic questions or frustrations in trying to deal with them. Something like that seems to have been happening in the congressional budget process. The new procedure established in 1974 reflected the belief that the previous, decentralized process did not sufficiently focus on the global issues like the size of the deficit or surplus, total expenditures, and total receipts. The new procedure presumably would force the Congress first to concentrate on the big issues and then to conform the details to the decisions on those issues. The budget committees and the two houses in acting on the budget resolutions, however, have become more and more concerned with the details, so that the aggregates are increasingly the consequence of the detailed decisions. This is probably because the connection between the global decisions and the global objectives is not seen to be so clear and compelling that the global decisions dominate the details.

There is thus an administrative management or information management problem of where to draw the line between macro-instruments and macro-objectives and microinstruments and micro-objectives. That is a question that every large organization faces. It does not seem to have been systematically studied for the U.S. budget. What is involved, of course, is not the academic question of dividing the college curriculum between fiscal policy and public finance. It is the practical question of getting the decisions made at the right level of government and in relation to the right objectives.

My suggestion above that macropolicy at the fiscal and real level would include several—say, six or seven—instruments and a similar number of objectives runs into another difficulty, which is political. The decisions obviously cannot be made by a computer. The relation between the instruments and the objectives is too uncertain, and the relative weight to be given to the several objectives is too much a matter of subjective evaluation for that. The decisions will have to be made by people and will reflect their estimates and value judgments. The question then is what people will make the decisions and what their biases will be.

It seems clear that if we have a decision process with six or seven instruments, the decisions will have to be made by living government officials—politicians—using their discretion. One can imagine a different procedure. Conceivably there could be a decision now that the budget should be balanced forever, that total expenditures and receipts should be 20 percent of GNP, transfer payments 10 percent of GNP, personal income tax 9 percent of GNP, and a few other numbers. All of this could be incorporated in the Constitution or, by a process of persuasion, made part of a durable national consensus. That would free those decisions from the biases of living, transient politicians. But no one proposes to go that far. Doing so would eliminate the possibility of taking advantage of new information as it becomes available or of responding to changing national preferences. For most of these decisions it would be universally agreed that the loss of information would outweigh the gain from avoiding transient bias. Moreover, one cannot be certain whether the constitutional amendment or moral rule about the budget avoids "bias" in the decisions or only substitutes the biases of dead politicians for those of living ones, or the biases of politicians out of office or going out for those of politicians in office or expecting to come in.

There may, however, be one or two decisions for which the elimination of what I will call contemporary bias (as distinguished from inherited bias) is much more important than adaptation to changing conditions, information, and priorities. The decision about the size of the budget deficit or surplus (the correct decision being assumed to be zero) is frequently considered to fall into this category. There are people who believe that the ratio of total government spending to GNP falls into this category (the proper ratio being a little lower than the ratio just reached).

The intent here is to emphasize the need to think about and try to reach agreement about how various budget decisions are made— at which level of government, by what procedures, in terms of what objectives, for what duration, and subject to what outside constraints. This problem is made exceedingly difficult by many considerations:

the budget consists of a number of policy instruments; there are a number of objectives; each objective is affected by several instruments, and many instruments affect several objectives; effects of the instruments on the objectives are hard to estimate; the relative values of the objectives are matters of personal preference, which change from time to time; and the instruments interact with each other, not least because the sources and uses of funds will be equal. But some intermediate practical ground must be sought, both for thinking and for acting, between trying to make all the decisions simultaneously and singling out individual decisions to be made in isolation.

It may be pointed out here that the problem of fixing some decisions for all time, or a very long time, and insulating them from contemporary politics is different in the monetary-nominal realm than in the fiscal-real realm. Possibly in some sense better monetary decisions would be made if they were flexibly adapted from quarter to quarter to changing conditions, information, and preferences. But the dominant objective of policy for the nominal world is not this adaptation but the creation of an environment in which the actors—individuals, business, and governments—can efficiently make their own adaptations. And the most important characteristic of that environment is constancy and predictability. For some aspects of the budget, constancy and predictability are also valuable. But they are not nearly as dominant over the need for adaptation as in the case of monetary policy. Budget policy *is* making decisions about the uses of the real output of the economy, not merely providing a "neutral" stage for making those decisions. To freeze those real decisions for any great length of time would be unrealistic, whereas freezing is the essence of good nominal decisions.

The Targets of Monetary Policy. The preceding discussion has assumed that monetary policy is aimed proximately at some variable in the nominal world—money supply, nominal GNP, the price level—with the expectation, of course, that a beneficial result for the real world will follow. This is to be distinguished from aiming directly at a real variable like the unemployment rate or real output or its rate of growth. Whether this assumption is correct or not is a critical question, which needs to be discussed. I believe that professional opinion is coming increasingly to this view, but there are still dissenters within the economics profession and probably more people outside the profession who still think in the other terms.

The experience of the past fifteen or twenty years seems to support strongly the idea of not aiming at a real target. During most of that period monetary policy has undertaken to achieve some rate of unemployment or has felt obliged to reduce the rate when it significantly exceeded some acceptable level. This policy has contributed to an acceleration of inflation, because the unemployment goal was consistently lower than could be achieved without accelerating inflation. The policy did not for long keep the unemployment rate at the target level, because the inflation rate that would have been necessary for this would have been unacceptable. Policy hovered between being expansive enough to keep unemployment low and being restrictive enough to keep inflation from accelerating. And now we face a painful and perhaps protracted period of unemployment in an effort to regain price-level stability.

Some would disagree with this diagnosis. They would argue that the problem was not in aiming at an unemployment target but in aiming at too ambitious an unemployment target. Economists work with a concept called the nonaccelerating inflation rate of unemployment (NAIRU), which is the lowest unemployment rate that would be experienced if the rate of inflation were stable. If monetary policy aimed to make the actual unemployment rate equal to the NAIRU—restricting when the actual was below NAIRU, and vice versa—there would be no tendency for inflation to accelerate.

The trouble is, of course, that no one knows what the NAIRU is at any moment. We have no way to measure it. All we can say is that NAIRU is the unemployment rate that would prevail if the inflation rate was stable for a considerable period and was expected to stay that way. So there is no reliable way to aim directly at the NAIRU. The best we can do is to aim at stabilizing the inflation rate and watching the NAIRU emerge. Moreover, it is extremely likely that if we try to aim directly at the NAIRU, we will in fact aim at too low a rate. Since no one can be sure what the NAIRU is, the political temptation will always be strong to aim at a low unemployment rate, because the inflationary consequences of that will come only after the passage of some time.

Moreover, it seems clear, as already noted, that if the immediate target is a nominal variable, the essential characteristic to be sought in the nominal variable is predictability. Fundamentally this is an argument for the predictability of the price level, although, as will be explained shortly, this does not necessarily mean that monetary policy should aim directly at the predictability of the price level. Individuals and businesses make decisions and commitments for the future in terms of dollars and with expectations of what the future real value of the dollar will be. Businesses and their employees enter into wage contracts in which both parties are estimating what the future value of the dollar will be. Businesses and their creditors make borrowing, lending, and investing decisions in the light of some expectations about the future value of the dollar. Uncertainty about the future value of the dollar is a burden on these decisions and makes investment and employment less than they would otherwise be. Moreover, if the actual value of the dollar turns out to be different from what had been expected, there are disappointments, unexpected changes in the distribution of income, shortages, and unemployment.

Predictability does not have to mean constancy. The time of sunrise changes from day to day but is perfectly predictable. That only means, of course, that there is a constant cycle through the year. But as a practical matter predictability of the price level will only be achieved with constancy of either the level or its rate of change. Moreover, since we are dealing with a predictability that is to be achieved by policy, there is no reason to make the predicted pattern more complicated than simple constancy. So I shall assume that we are considering a monetary policy aimed at achieving stability in the level or rate of change of a nominal variable.

A number of questions then arise. The first is, What should be the nominal variable at which monetary policy should aim? There are a number of possibilities:

- "the" price level (or "a" price index, there being many)
- nominal GNP
- some measure of the money supply, such as M1 or M2
- the monetary base—bank reserves plus currency in circulation—which limits the supply of money
- the price of gold
- interest rates

The previous discussion might seem to have made it obvious that the price level is the proper target of monetary policy. Predictability of the price level is what we are after as a condition in which economic decisions will yield their best results because expectations about the value of money will come true. So one might think that monetary policy should be directed toward stabilizing the price level or its rate of inflation, with the monetary authority (the Federal Reserve) accelerating or decelerating the growth of the money supply as it considers appropriate for achieving the desired behavior of the price level.

This formulation immediately reveals one critical difficulty with use of the price level as the target. The instruction to the Federal Reserve would be that it should accelerate or decelerate growth of the money supply "as it considers appropriate." But the acceleration or deceleration of growth that is appropriate would not be known objectively and precisely. The Federal Reserve would have to use its discretion in managing the money supply. Moreover, one could not tell after the fact whether departures of the price level from its target path were the result of honest and inevitable errors or showed that the Federal Reserve was not following its instructions. That is, it would be difficult to maintain accountability and check a bias that would probably be in the inflationary direction.

The first four possible targets listed above are ranked in a certain hierarchical order. The price level is the most relevant target—that is, its predictability would yield the most of what we would like to achieve. Controllability and accountability are least, however, if the price level is the target. At the other extreme, the monetary base is the variable most controllable by the Federal Reserve, and the Federal Reserve could most clearly be held responsible for departures from the desired path of the base. But the predictability of the base would contribute least to the efficient operation of the economy because individuals and businesses do not make decisions on the basis of their expectations about the base.

These four targets are causally linked to one another. The growth of the base controls the growth of the money supply, but with some looseness and uncertainty in the linkage. The growth of the money supply controls the growth of nominal GNP, but with some looseness and uncertainty in the linkage. The growth of nominal GNP controls the rate of inflation, but again with some looseness and uncertainty in the linkage.

If the linkages were tight and well known, the choice among these four targets would make no difference. Targeting on the base would yield the desired behavior of the price level. Targeting on the price level would indicate precisely what had to be done about the base. The choice of the target depends on two factors—the looseness of the linkage and the risk of bias that emerges when accountability is weak. If the linkage is close but the risk of bias great, it may be worthwhile to aim at the base, or the money supply, even at the sacrifice of some relevance. Or some intermediate position might be optimum. The money supply might be a better target than the base, for example, if the link between the base and the money supply was loose while the link between the money supply and the price level was tight.

There are two other reasons, probably less important, why the price level may not be the best target. One is that we mean by the price level the price at which, on the average, goods and services can be bought and sold. The price index may not measure that very well in some circumstances. The main case is that in times of recession, when demand declines, prices are sticky, and it is not true that the volume of goods and services that would be supplied at the quoted prices can be sold at those prices.

A second problem results from what are now called supply shocks. Suppose that the target is 2 percent per year inflation and that real growth nominally goes on at 3 percent per year, so that nominal GNP is rising by 5 percent per year. If there is a temporary interruption of some important supply, such as an oil embargo, so that real growth falls to 1 percent per year, the inflation rate will rise to 4 percent if the growth of nominal GNP remains unchanged. To hold the inflation rate constant at 2 percent would require a very prompt contraction of the growth of nominal GNP, and that would almost certainly cause a sharp contraction of real output. A policy of stabilizing the growth rate of nominal GNP would avoid or moderate the secondary contractions of real output, but would also permit the price level to deviate for a period from the desired path.

There has been a good deal of recent interest in using nominal GNP as a target of monetary policy, and not only for the reason just cited. Nominal GNP is intermediate among the possible goals. It is closer to what we are really interested in—the price level—than the money supply or base money, and it is quite unlikely that the inflation rate could accelerate markedly if the growth rate of nominal GNP were stabilized. At the same time, it is probably more controllable than the price level itself.

The choice among the hierarchy of targets is best looked at as a question of deciding the period to which the targets refer, rather than as a question of choosing one target to the exclusion of the others. That is, there have to be targets for all four variables all the time, and the issue is how frequently, or on what evidence, the targets are to be changed. Suppose, for example, we decide that the monetary base should be the target. How would we decide what the height of the target should be—whether, for example, we should aim at constancy of the monetary base or a 3 percent per year increase? Presumably we would have to go through a thinking process about the relation between the base and the price level. We might say that our basic goal is that the price level should be stable. We estimate that the normal growth of real output is 3 percent per year. Therefore, to keep the price level stable we need a 3 percent per year increase of nominal GNP. We estimate that velocity increases by 1 percent per year, so that to get nominal GNP rising by 3 percent, we need the money supply growing by 2 percent. Finally, we estimate that the money supply rises at the same rate as the monetary base— the "base multiplier" is one—so that to have the money supply rising by 2 percent per year, the monetary base must rise by 2 percent per year.

Thus the target for the monetary base is derived from a target for the price level, through estimates of real growth, velocity, and the base multiplier. But these estimates are only estimates. They can be wrong in the short run or in the long run. If they are wrong, the desired levels of the four targets will not all be achieved at once. The choice of "the" target is a decision about what will be adapted first if some adaptation is necessary. If the monetary base is "the" target, the other variables will be allowed to deviate from their expected and desired path until strong evidence, probably accumulated over some period of time, shows the need to change the path of the monetary base. If, for example, nominal GNP is "the" target, this would imply, through estimates of velocity and of the base multiplier, targets for the money supply and for base money. But saying that nominal GNP is "the" target implies that if these estimates of velocity and the base multiplier turn out to be incorrect, the base multiplier and the money supply will be adapted in an effort to keep nominal GNP on its path, rather than the other way around.

I have elsewhere suggested one approach to the problem of ordering the targets. We might say that our long-term goal is an inflation rate of 2 percent per year. We could then decide that for a period of, say, five years we would aim at nominal GNP growing by 5 percent per year, on an estimate that real output would grow by 3 percent per year. But we could revise this nominal growth target every five years if there was strong reason to believe that 3 percent was not the normal growth rate of real output. Each year the Federal Reserve would set a target for the growth of the money supply, calculated to achieve the nominal GNP growth target. This involves a forecast of velocity. The Federal Reserve could revise the target rate for money growth each year as necessary to get on the nominal GNP growth path. Moreover, the growth of the monetary base could be more or less continuously adapted to try to achieve the desired growth of the money supply.

A more sophisticated and cautious version of this approach has been suggested by William Fellner. He believes that the relation between the monetary base and nominal GNP can be reasonably well predicted from one business cycle to another. Therefore, he would fix the rate of growth of the monetary base for each entire business cycle to achieve the desired course of nominal GNP over the entire cycle. But he believes that the relation between the monetary base and nominal GNP is not sufficiently predictable during the cycle to justify the attempt to vary the base in an effort to offset cyclical or random fluctuations in the relation. That is, he believes that keeping constant the rate of growth of the monetary base during the period of each business cycle will achieve as much stability of nominal GNP within the cycle as is achievable and will reduce the danger of cumulative errors that might lead to accelerating inflation or deflation.

Again I am not proposing either of the answers to the question of monetary strategy, but only trying to illustrate what the question is. Although there has been much study of this subject in the past twenty years, there is still disagreement among experts on the targets of monetary policy. Neither can it be said to be settled what the policy of the Federal Reserve now is. Although the Federal Reserve is said to take the growth of the money supply as its target, this leaves a great many uncertainties. The Federal Reserve sets the target for monetary growth each year and sometimes revises the target at the midyear point. But it has not committed itself to any longer-run path with respect to either the price level or nominal GNP, although it is believed to be aiming at something with respect to these two variables. Thus not only do we not know what the money supply targets are beyond the next twelve months (or less), we do not even know what the Federal Reserve will be thinking about or aiming at when it does set the next year's money supply target. Moreover, the annual targets are set in terms of a wide range for the permissible growth of the money supply and also in terms of at least two definitions of the money supply, which often point in different directions. And there is uncertainty about what the policy of the Federal Reserve will be if the actual money supply runs outside the target range. Observers do not know whether such a development foretells action to get down within the target range or signifies a change in the target range. There is still doubt about the most critical question, which is whether the Federal Reserve still has in mind some real targets, such as the unemployment rate.

Because the Federal Reserve has not been more explicit about its strategy, it has not gained the results in predictability and credibility that it undoubtedly sought when it made what it regarded as a major turn to anti-inflationary policy in 1979. It will not be sufficient, however, for the Federal Reserve to clarify its policy, important as that would be. It will be necessary for the policy to be endorsed by the other actors in the making of monetary policy—the administration and the Congress—and to be understood in the private sector.

Only a few words need to be said about two other possible targets that have recently attracted attention. One is to stabilize the price of gold. The rationale for this proposal is the belief that the real price of gold tends to be stable—that is, the price of gold moves in parallel with the price level. If that relation remains constant, stabilizing the price of gold will stabilize the general price level, but the underlying premise about the stability of the relationship is not sufficiently reliable to be the basis of monetary policy. This was the conclusion of a recent examination of the subject by a government commission. This question is analyzed further in Phillip Cagan's *Current Problems of Monetary Policy: Would the Gold Standard Help?*

The other recent, or revived, proposal is that monetary policy should be used to stabilize interest rates. This proposal can only be attributed to confusion and ignorance of history. During World War II and until 1951 we had such a policy in the United States. Experience and argument at that time demonstrated that the policy was a prescription for endless inflation. Inflation tended to raise interest rates, and under the policy the tendency for interest rates to rise had to be countered by expansion of the money supply, which raised inflation further, tending to raise interest rates further and thus requiring more monetary expansion, and so on.

Whatever target is chosen for monetary policy, a decision has to be made about what the rate of growth of the target variable should be. As has already been said several times, the fundamental consideration is that the rate of growth should be predictable. Whether the annual rate of increase of the price level is zero or 10 percent does not in principle seem to be very important if the two rates are equally predictable.

The problem has to be seen in historical perspective. We have been going through fifteen years of accelerating inflation. We have labor contracts, credit contracts, and less formal arrangements that reflect the expectation of a high rate of inflation—say, 8 percent. If monetary policy were to aim now at getting the inflation rate promptly to zero—or to a target for the money supply consistent with that— there would be losses and unemployment for some people in the process. Thus there seems to be a case for stabilizing the inflation rate where it is, and there are supporters of this idea.

But such a policy may not achieve the predictability that is desired. It may be interpreted as signifying that if the inflation rate rises, as a result of errors of policy or exogenous forces, the Federal Reserve will then attempt to stabilize the rate of inflation at its new level. This will lead to the expectation of an inflation rate that continues to ratchet upward, as it has done in the recent past. There will be much uncertainty about the rate at which this happens and occasional temporary bouts of disinflation. This would not be the path of predictability that is sought.

So there seems to be a choice between trying to stabilize the high rates of growth of money, nominal GNP, and the price level already achieved and getting back down to a lower level more consistent with price-level stability. This choice depends on the painfulness of getting down and the feasibility of staying up without further escalation. Choosing the policy of getting down opens up the question of the rate at which this is to be done. That is a question largely disregarded in the discussion of monetary stabilization, which tends to focus on the virtue of keeping to a low rate of inflation that has somehow been achieved and to ignore the problem of a transition to that point from a more inflationary one.

There are two main options for this transition—cold turkey and gradualism. Where this choice has been presented, the answer has always been for gradualism. Although there has been no rigorous demonstration that gradualism is the less costly solution, it does seem to be the less risky solution, or at least the solution with less immediate risks. But gradualism, even if it is accepted, is not a precise term and encompasses a considerable range of speeds of disinflation. The importance of this question was highlighted in 1981–1982. There was, at least for a time, a faster deceleration of money growth than many people, including the administration, expected, and a faster deceleration of inflation. This was accompanied by a bigger rise of unemployment than had been expected. But it was not clear whether this was to be considered a desirable course, to be continued, or whether it was an overshooting of the disinflationary process, to be compensated for subsequently by more expansionary policy. This question became acute in the summer of 1982, when unemployment reached 10 percent, and it was not obvious what answer the Federal Reserve gave to it. More explicit discussion of this question and agreement on it, especially between the administration and the Federal Reserve, is needed.

The Principles of Stabilizing Fiscal Policy

I have stated above my belief that, with one exception, fiscal policy should be regarded as dealing with the real economy, rather than with nominal variables and those aspects of real economic behavior that are mainly determined by the nominal variables. The exception was that year-to-year stability in fiscal policy as it affects the nominal variables is desirable. This view is based on the belief that monetary policy could compensate for any effects of fiscal policy on nominal demand and on those variables that are affected by nominal demand if the effects of fiscal policy were predictable and stable.

The general separation between fiscal policy and the management of aggregate nominal demand is, of course, like other suggestions advanced here, put forward as a question deserving study and decision. I shall proceed here, however, on the assumption that this idea is accepted.

The first question that arises is how to describe a policy that stabilizes the effect of the budget on the nominal variables, by which I mean nominal demand or nominal GNP. There are two problems here: how to measure the effect of the budget and how to distinguish the effect of the budget on nominal GNP from the effect of nominal GNP on the budget.

With respect to the first problem, one can imagine assigning multipliers for the effect on nominal GNP of each particular tax, expenditure, or means of borrowing—different multipliers for each—and adding up to get a weighted total effect. But while one can imagine that, one cannot do it. We do not know enough to do that with any reliability. That is, we do not know enough to be confident that this weighted multiplier would be a more reliable indicator of the total effect than would some cruder measure, such as the size of the deficit or surplus.

There may be some intermediate practice between trying to assign different multipliers to each expenditure and receipt, on the one hand, and looking only at the deficit or surplus, on the other hand, which would give a better measure of the net effect on aggregate demand. The textbooks suggest, for example, that expenditures for the purchase of goods and services should have a higher weight than transfer payments and tax receipts. My own view is that the gain in precision is not worth the complexity introduced, especially if we are concerned with measuring the change in effect between one year and another within short periods, where the composition of the budget in these terms is not likely to change much. That is, however, an empirical question, which deserves further study.

Even if we are going to use the size of the deficit or surplus as the measure of net effect on aggregate demand, the problem of weights arises in the definition of the budget. Since sources and uses of funds will be equal, for the federal government as for other entities, the notion of a deficit or surplus implies giving a weight of one to some sources and uses and a weight of zero to others. The chief relevance of that at present is the treatment of loan transactions, some of which are officially given a weight of one and included in the budget and others given a weight of zero and called off-budget. Many unofficial observers of budget policy do not accept this and include the off-budget transactions in their conception of the budget and the deficit. For the moment this does not matter much, since with or without the "off-budget" items the deficits are commonly agreed to be "outrageously" high. But the question of definition would become more significant as we approached an acceptable budget position. My preference would be to exclude all loan transactions from the budget, both those that are now included in the budget and those that are "off-budget." I believe that government lending and borrowing are closer to debt transactions than to expenditure transactions. That is, however, also an empirical question, which needs to be studied.

A larger question is how we would define stability of whatever measure we accept as the indicator of aggregate demand effect—presumably the budget deficit or surplus. The economy fluctuates in response to many variables outside the budget, and the deficit or surplus fluctuates in response to such fluctuations of the economy. Fluctuations arising in this way do not reflect changes in the aggregate-demand effect of the budget. There is, I suppose, common agreement that attempting to offset such fluctuations by changing tax rates or expenditure programs is neither necessary nor desirable.

The problem is how to distinguish these passive changes in the budget position from other changes that do actively disturb the aggregate-demand situation. The answer to that is to calculate the budget position (deficit or surplus) as it would be at some standard stable, or steadily growing, condition of the economy and to consider the budget to be in a stable position if this hypothetical deficit or surplus is stable. That is what the notion of balancing the budget (actually, in the first formulation, running a small surplus) at high employment did. There turned out to be serious difficulties with that formulation. First, no one knew what "high employment" was, and second, this formulation assumed away the problem of inflation. Yet the basic idea incorporated there was sound, even though the particular formulation was rather primitive. The idea was that we wanted to stabilize the budget position as it would be under desirable, feasible, and probable conditions of the economy. To aim at stabilizing the budget position under conditions that were not desirable or not feasible or not probable would not yield desired results from any standpoint. The strategy implicit in the idea was that monetary policy would aim at achieving the feasible, desirable aggregate conditions, that fiscal policy could be based on the assumption that the monetary policy would be successful on the average, though not in every year, and that fiscal policy could be directed to achieving its desired results under those conditions and in a way that would at least not disrupt the efforts of monetary policy and might assist them. Thus there would be a complementarity of fiscal and monetary policies. Monetary policy would make the feasible and desirable conditions probable. A fiscal policy that would keep the budget position stable under these probable conditions would at least not interfere with the achievement of this goal of monetary policy and would tend to achieve in actuality whatever were the goals of fiscal policy itself.

The prescription that the budget should be set so as to balance at high employment was, as it turned out, a crude expression of that theory. The original formulation of the Committee for Economic Development, in 1947, recognized the price-level problem, but not the magnitude it would actually take, and offered no formula for handling it. Implicitly, the fiscal policy assumed that the monetary policy would succeed in stabilizing the price level. If monetary policy did not do that—as, of course, it did not—then the fiscal policy would not yield the results its developers sought from it.

As for fiscal policy, the basic proposition is that it should stabilize its outcome—presumably the size of the budget surplus or deficit—as it would be if the economy moved along the path at which monetary policy is aiming. This requires, since fiscal policy has to be planned for several years in advance, that the targets of monetary policy be specified for some years in advance and that these targets be agreed to by both the fiscal authorities and the monetary authority. This relation between fiscal policy and monetary policy requires that the monetary target either be nominal GNP or be translatable into nominal GNP, because the nominal GNP is a necessary ingredient for calculating the revenue and expenditure consequences of tax and expenditure programs. That is, one could not calculate what the revenues, expenditures, and surplus results would be under assumed conditions of the money supply or of the monetary base without first estimating what nominal GNP would be under those monetary conditions.

Of course, this kind of fiscal policy does not assume that monetary policy achieves its targets year by year but only that it does so on the average over a longer period. It is only the recognition that the actual path of the economy will deviate from the target path that requires the calculation of hypothetical budgets and the prescription of budget goals in terms of these hypothetical calculations.

This whole approach to the budget through calculation of hypothetical outcomes has commonly been rejected by "practical" people. They have regarded it as an evasion or gimmick to escape the hard requirements of actually balancing the budget, and they have dismissed the calculations of "high employment" budgets as mere dreaming or fakery. They insist, as a secretary of the treasury once said, on "balancing the budget, period." This issue will have to be faced. The practical people will have to recognize that "balancing the budget, period" is the least practical of all the possibilities. Budgeting is planning for the future, and while policies can be decided in advance, the outcome of those policies cannot be told in advance. The policy decisions will have to be made on the basis of predictions of their outcomes, which depend on unforeseeable developments in the future state of the economy. The only question is what should be assumed about the future when the decisions are made. The proposition advanced here is that the path of the economy that is the target of monetary policy is both the most probable path and the path that fiscal policy should be most careful not to disturb and therefore the path on which it is most meaningful to stabilize the budget position. This subject requires much more explicit discussion than it has recently had. Nothing could be more obvious than that much current talk about deficits is made meaningless by failure to specify the conditions under which the deficits are assumed to be incurred.

The idea that the budget position should be stable, so as to avoid disrupting the efforts of monetary policy, does not imply that it should be constant forever. It only means that it should change infrequently and should not change abruptly or unpredictably from year to year. It would not, for example, be inconsistent with deciding that the budget deficit should be gradually reduced as the economy moves along a path to low inflation and high employment and that the deficit should then settle down at a low level—not necessarily zero. Neither would it be inconsistent with a decision, at some later date, that the deficit should settle for some extended period at some larger number or, alternatively, at zero.

Stability of the hypothetical, or target, deficit or surplus would be the contribution of fiscal policy to the stability of aggregate demand and to the effectiveness of monetary policy. The level at which the deficit or surplus is stable would be determined by considerations other than aggregate demand, considerations that presumably change slowly and do not require frequent changes in the overall fiscal target.[1]

Real Fiscal Policy

The preceding discussion narrows the stabilization function of fiscal policy to serving as a rather minor and passive adjunct of monetary policy. Not everyone may accept this "demotion" of fiscal policy. But no one can deny that a major, and possibly dominant, function of fiscal policy is found in another arena—namely, in the allocation of the national output among alternative uses and persons. This is, we are increasingly coming to recognize, as true of the deficit or surplus as it is of expenditures for defense or for aid to families with dependent children. The deficit or surplus is a way of allocating the national output between investment and consumption.

I have considered above whether there is any "macro" aspect to this function of fiscal policy. Are we required, or permitted, to consider each of several thousand microdecisions about the budget in comparison with each of the several thousand other microdecisions? I have answered that question in the negative, on the ground that we do not have the information that would make it possible to answer all the questions simultaneously and that it would not be politically acceptable to do so even if it were possible. We must organize the decisions in the budget according to their degree of importance and generality, with higher-level, more responsible officials making the more general and important decisions and lower-level officials making the lesser decisions within the limits set by the more general decisions. The classification of these decisions and their assignment to levels of government is one of the key issues of budget policy.

A related question is whether there is any "economics" to the real budgetary decisions, however macro or micro those decisions are considered to be. There are two kinds of issues involved in these decisions. One is the issue of values. How much does the society value, for example, efficiency or growth in comparison with equality or justice? A similar question can be asked about the value to be attached to degrees of freedom from national security risks. These are not questions that economists or other social scientists should be expected or trusted to answer, although they do seem quite prepared to offer answers.

The other kind of issue is more instrumental. It is a matter of assessing or predicting the results of actual or proposed policies in terms of the objectives we are interested in. How much difference for the rate of economic growth would result from the difference between balancing the budget and running a deficit of $100 billion a year? How much difference would it make if the top marginal rate of income tax were 30 percent rather than 50 percent? How much more education would result from another $10 billion of federal aid to education, how much additional competence would result from that, and how much additional productivity and national output would result from that additional competence? How much do transfer payments reduce poverty, and how much do they increase dependency?

These are questions on which economists and other social scientists ought, in principle, to be able to throw light. That is, they are not just questions of preferences and tastes, about which disputes and investigations are ruled out. But the fact is that we do not know much about them. The situation can be put more precisely. We do not know nearly as much about these questions as we would like to know, but we know more about many of them than is reflected in public discussion and in the policy-making process.

The 1981 supply-side tax cut is the most obvious example of this situation. It is perfectly true that economists did not know with any precision what the size and timing of the effects of the tax cuts on incentives to work and save would be. Still, the argument made for the tax cut, and probably the reasons that supported it in the minds of many people, implied that these effects would be of a size and speed quite outside the range that economists would have considered probable.

Similar observations, though less clear-cut, can be made about other major fiscal decisions. Economists and other social scientists would probably agree, for example, that they can estimate only crudely and uncertainly the effects of government antipoverty programs on poverty, dependency, and other conditions of national concern. But the popular and political discussion of such programs commonly implies judgments about these effects, positive and negative, that are outside the range within which experts would think the truth lies.

There is little that can be said here about how to make better decisions on the real aspects of fiscal policy. Obviously, we need to learn more. Students of fiscal policy have had an excursion for about fifty years in the field of nominal macroeconomics. It is time now to devote more attention to the real side of things—to the effects of budget decisions on the allocation of the national output. That has already begun, but it needs to be carried much further.

But at best we will learn slowly. We will have to make decisions with inadequate information, and for a long time we will not have much more information than we now have. The problem of government policy will be, as always, what to do when you don't know what to do—when the available information does not point unequivocally to a certain policy as best. There is no specific prescription for handling this problem. The answer lies in the qualities that are generally described as sound judgment and responsibility. There are some rules of thumb that suggest elements of what is required: policy should not change in big leaps unless there are unusual and radical changes in conditions; "try and see" is a good rule; the lessons of experience should be studied; political consensus should be respected, and the squeaking wheel should get the grease; if it ain't broke, don't fix it. To spell out a prescription for sound judgment and responsible behavior is obviously beyond the scope of this paper and the competence of this author. But to recognize what we don't know, and what we must think about, is a step toward better decisions, and it is hoped that this paper is a contribution toward that.

December 1982

Note

1. In its 1947 policy statement, *Taxes and the Budget,* the Research and Policy Committee of the Committee for Economic Development recommended that taxes be set so as to yield a moderate surplus and kept there "unless there is a major change in the conditions of national life." This final clause was a Keynesian escape hatch, in case it turned out that at some future time the achievement of high employment would be incompatible with a moderate budget deficit. I am not suggesting that we need a Keynesian escape hatch. I am suggesting that the considerations determining the proper size of the deficit or surplus are not constant forever.

Studies in
CONTEMPORARY ECONOMIC PROBLEMS, 1982

STANLEY W. BLACK — Politics versus Markets: International Differences in Macroeconomic Policies

PHILLIP CAGAN — Current Problems of Monetary Policy: Wou[ld] the Gold Standard Help?

BARRY R. CHISWICK — The Employment of Immigrants in the Unit[ed] States

WILLIAM FELLNER — The High Employment Budget and Potenti[al] Output: A Critique Focusing on Two Rece[nt] Contributions

D. GALE JOHNSON — Progress of Economic Reform in the People['s] Republic of China

JOHN W. KENDRICK — Interindustry Differences in Productivi[ty] Growth

MARK PERLMAN — Patterns of Regional Economic Decline a[nd] Growth: The Past and What Has Been Ha[p]pening Lately

HERBERT STEIN — Agenda for the Study of Macroeconom[ic] Policy

Comments on previous volumes:

• *". . . continues to provide informative reading on a wide ran[ge] of important issues for professional economists and policy makers[.]"*

• *"Overall, this is a useful volume for teachers and students [of] macroeconomic policy."*

JOURNAL OF ECONOMIC LITERATU[RE]

American Enterprise Institute for Public Policy Researc[h] 1150 Seventeenth Street, N.W., Washington, D.C. 2003[6]